...ction

...ouse where I spent my school days. The family home had a personality of its own consisting of nine rooms from cellar to attic or study. Each room had a purpose and hold lots of wonderful memories. Rooms were also a great place to think or hide and when you had a room or rooms to yourself it was extra special and magical even if you had been sent there.

Each room was a place of comfort and refuge and had its own story to share about you or with you.

I also loved my parent's Jamaican accent, and still do. It was very similar to the English I learned at school. Although it was a type of English, it was called Patois. They spoke quicker and more expressively than most of my teachers. They also spoke a lot of traditional Jamaican proverbs, which stretched our imagination working them out. I suppose they got them from their parents and these are handed down to us as I try to share some of them with you.

I hope you also see the wisdom and humour to be found in Jamaican proverbs. There are proverbs from all different cultures that are just as interesting. I'm sure you can spend some time finding some proverbs for yourself. Tell them to family and friends whenever you think the time is purposeful, as there is a lot of wisdom and knowledge to be found in proverbs.

....

As my father would say,
"a nuh everyting weh sink float straight away".
Which means success or failure doesn't happen overnight.
Or when dawg flea bite yu, yu afi cratch.
Every action will cause some kind of reaction.

And once you start to go through this Book of Rooms
I'm sure you will see.
This is true.

Dedications and Blessings
To
Thoughtfulness, Kindliness, Essence,
T'naya, Kayon, Elijah,

And, of course, yourself.

Bless you all in all you do,
And all who reside or sail with you.

Contents of the Apartments

Welcome To The
PEN-TASTIC
APARTMENT

To put your feet up for your leisure...

READ AND SEEK

In my book, and don't be scared; to take a little look.
Read and seek to explore your mind.
And don't be afraid of what you'll find.

Turn and read the pages and in between the lines.
Comprehend and understand, so roll up your blinds.
Every letter builds a word that should be defined.
Some time you got to stop and let time rewind.

Rrr ruh ruh ruh ruh ruh ruh ruh ruh REWIND.
As something that you missed; should have truly
been defined
So you've got to stop living behind those blinds,
And methodically start; to read all those lines.

Read and seek in my book,
Even if you're hard and very tuff.
Read and seek and know your stuff.
It seems every day you're in such a big huff.

Seek and read, just look for the jewel,
Then no one can take you for a Tom fool.
Learn to read yo start at school;
Reading can become a life saving tool.

Now go and read a book yo,
Start one today.
And if you can't read; you only have to say.
I'd like to read a book, all by myself;
But today I could do with a little bit a help.

Read and seek in my book,
And don't be scared to take a little look.
Read and seek to explore your mind.
I'm sure you'll be amazed at what you find.

A FLOWIT

Thinks about things on their mind,
Then just flows and makes all things rhyme.
A flowit can have a steely stare,
As they concentrate on what is there.
If it's books, pens, pencil, sandpaper,
It all flows out just like data.
Morning, evening, noon or nights,
He likes to flow b4 he writes.
Flowing, yowing like a rollercoaster,
Busting out rhymez like he's supposed ta.
Flowing with reality, sometimes with insanity,
But never with profanity.
From heaven to earth and the deep-blue sea,
Rhymez are there for all to see.
Concentrate and flow with me,
Every word you speak is poetry.
A flowit is a flowit and I want you to know it,
A flowit is a poet like you and me.

ALL MI FACTS

Yow! I wanna do a rap and a wanna do it fast,
So I'll grab all mi facts and put dem in mi raps.

Like Olaudah Equiano was eleven years old.
When he was captured then got sold.
Port Royal sank with pirates' gold.
King Shaka Zulu was brave and bold.
And if you stare at gold you might go blind.
It's just like looking into bright sunshine.

So all of mi raps go rapper rap tat,
I chat dem slow and I blather dem fast,
I build concrete raps that are built to last,
That tell you bout the future, and tell you bout the past.

I wanna do a rap and a wanna do it fast,
So I'll grab all mi facts and put dem in mi raps.

Even when my headz in bed.
Rhymez keep surfing in my head.
Like always think before speak.
And your words will be iron and full of concrete.
I wanna do a rap and a wanna do it fast,
So I'll grab all mi facts and put dem in mi raps.
But if they don't know the argument or even the facts,
Then maybe you suggest they shut their traps.

Note: Jamaican proverb:
Nuh drive fly from a next man cow skin. =
Never interfere with other people's business.

AN ATTIC FULL OF BOXES

With an attic full of boxes you can't even hoover,
You cannot sweep you cannot clean you can't even
manoeuvre.
With an attic full of boxes, things are very hard to find.
Even though they're all above, it seems I'm going blind.

The attic full of boxes has got to be unpacked,
But before I can do that, they have to be unstacked.

These boxes in the attic, you must have seen before,
Unpacking all these boxes has got to be a chore.
There's paper stuff to be done.
Surely must be not lots of fun.
Clutters and caroches must be removed.
More head space to be improved.
Out with the old then in with the new.
The boxes in the attic are things for me and you,
I'm sure you've got some boxes if you have a look too.

Those boxes are yours,
And these boxes are mine.
I'm sure you'll get to open up your boxes sometime.
Those boxes in the attic are things you may have left.
And some of them are simply jobs you haven't done yet.
The attic full of boxes is always on my mind.
But now I think it's the day, to find a little time.

Those boxes in the attic you always take to bed.
As these boxes in your attic;
You'll find them in your head!

Note: Caroches = odds and ends of personal belongings

CALLING RAPPAMAN

Rap rap Rappaman, Calling Rappaman.
It's the voice that you hear, when your head is in your hands.
Rap rap Rappaman, flash star bright,
Focus on solutions and things will be right.

Don't focus on the problem when it's already there.
Dilute it with solutions and wash it from your hair.
When you have a problem and you feel you can't cope.
There are always elucidations to bring a little hope.
So open up your eyes and read between the lines.
And you don't have to click your heels three times.

Rap rap Rappaman, Calling Rappaman.
It's the voice that you hear, when your head is in your hands.
Rap, rap, Rappaman, flash star bright,
Focus on solutions and things will be right.

Why? What? Who?
There are so many questions.
Anybody out there with any good suggestions
For the leaders of the world to change their directions?
Stop corruption and hidden agendas.
We gonna be a planet that no one remembers.
Blazing up in smoke like the fifth of Novembers.
This be for real, we ain't no pretenders.

Rap rap Rappaman, Calling Rappaman.
It's the voice that you hear, when your head is in your hand.
Rap rap Rappaman, flash star bright,
Focus on solutions and turn on the light!

*Note: Sometimes time is the only solution to make things
feel better. And remember, nothing can be done
before the time...*

THE BIG BAD BOOK

{Children can join in at the Big Bad Book hook / chorus}

How could a cool dude act so rude?
His manner was crude, and left you in a bad mood.
How could a real dude never learn to read?
When a book is the only friend they'll need.

Some boys are hard, girls ruff and tuff.
Full of ifs and full of buts.
Acting krazy and acting nuts.
My edz a shed but theirs are huts.

Don't be afraid of THE BIG BAD BOOK!
Why be afraid to tek a likkle look?
Everyone who reads can get stuck.
So don't be afraid of THE BIG BAD BOOK!

Books are there for you to learn.
And help you with the bucks you earn.
Books will help your mind get strong.
To know what's right, when you know what's wrong.
Books will help your knowledge to grow.
Just like a seed that you plant or sow.
Take some time to read a cool book.
And don't be like a Captain Hook.

Don't be afraid of THE BIG BAD BOOK!
Why be afraid to tek a likkle look?
Everyone who reads can get stuck,
So don't be afraid of THE BIG BAD BOOK!

Reading and writing is good for you.
It's good for tea and good for two.
Please learn to read, so you can understand.
You'll need these skills to grow to be a man.

A woman yes, it's good for you too.
Now you should know just what to do.
Gwarn now, grab yourself a book.
And call to a friend if you cl-ever get stuck.
Read a good book then come back and teach.
Never miss an opportunity even on the beach.

Every paragraph, letter, sentence and word
Will flow through your mind and should be observed.
Peep inside and stretcher-size your mind.
Comprehend what you read; discuss what you find.
If someone is trying to help you read.
Then that's the only type Book! that you'll need.
Reading's cool and reading's fun,
So help someone to get a book done.

Don't be afraid of THE BIG BAD BOOK!
Why be afraid to tek a likkle look?
Everyone who reads can get stuck,
So don't be afraid of THE BIG BAD BOOK!

Note: Likkle = Little} Gwarn = Go on}
Dude = Informal chap/ dandy

THE FIRST KING OF RAP

He was a raptor.
His teeth were full of bling, he was a cool actor.
With a yo and a SPLAT and a Prap Prap Brap!
Respect mi lyrics,
Him seh risspek dat.

When he rapped all the cavemen laughed.
But as soon as he finished, they all began to clap.
He said P to the R to the A to the P.
Please risspek all property.
P – R – A – P.
I threw this in to sting like a bee.
R to the A to the double P.
Risspek all people properly.

Now everyone knows he's a real smooth dapper.
And from his ends he's the very first rapper.
His next stage show yo is right up in Napa.
At a local club by the name of Mappa.
Then he'll tek a little trip down into rattery.
You know he's got a gig in a bread factory.
To an audience of mice and tuff ally cats.
Who began to shout and cheer when they heard his raps.
I'm the rap rap rappster.
A street news caster.
I rap a little faster.
The real word master.
A lyrical blaster.
To fix a disaster.
And just like a Rasta,
Spreading peace and love.

The first king of rap, he was a raptor.
His teeth were full of bling, he was a cool actor.
With a yo and a SPLAT and a Prap Prap Brap!
Respect mi lyrics,
Him seh risspek dat!

Note: Bling = gold or silver trinkets} Dat = that} and Seh = say} Rasta = a peace-loving person living a humble way of life and praising Jah/God and his works.

PEN-TASTIC

How many words can live in a pen?
Can't you count, ask a friend.
It's not one or two,
Five or ten,
You should know it's all of them.
Like,
Abigail Billal Claude Den
Elijah Frazier Gladissen
Hadji Ibrahim Jagdeep Kayon
Lloyd Merriam Niche Oman
Pablo Queenie Ritchie Steve
T'naya Uzman Valarie Wayne
Xavi Yolanda and even Zane.
From A to Zed it's so insane!

Ideas can roll out alphabetic.
Pens write them down so you don't forget it.

My pen stretches words more than elastic.
And writes from here to the cold Antarctic.
Across the equator and the greater Atlantic
It attracts the words just like a magnet.
And then on paper begins to splash it.
So your mind can see and even catch it.

That's why I got to shout about it.
The only way I can describe it.
Is to write it, scribe it and energise it
So all your vibes can utilise it.
Match it, flash it and even scratch it.
I've been told it's bold and big bombastic.
And dances on paper more like a gymnastic.
And since its invention I can't live without it.

But to me my pen's
Just
PEN-TASTIC.

CARNIVAL TIME

Carnival Carnival go wid di flow.
Sunshine, Sunshine there isn't no snow.

Let's dance and shout
Jump to the beat.
Join the parade out on the street.

If you're hungry there's plenty nuff food.
Fill up your belly; puts you in the right mood.
Chicken and spice all things nice.
Cold drinks, hot drinks and drinks with ice.

Costumes for fun an mask to wear.
Jump and shout like u just don't care.
Carnival Carnival let's have a good time.
Street people dancing all in a line.

Steel band playing lots of sounds,
Sound systems pump bass underground.

Pull up mi selector play it one more tiiiime,
Mi love di tune so me a beg a rewind.
Lots of children all blowing horns,
Adults eating fish an hot roast corn.
Carnival Carnival go wid di flow,
The carnival queen, she's on show.
Decorated in colours, while some in calico,
As she dance to di riddims of di Calypso.

Carnival Carnival roll wid di flow.
And now I'm feeling sad, as we've got to go.
But tomorrow I'll practise my Calypso,
Because this year I thought my moves were too slow.

3 JAMAICAN MICE

Sing!
Three Jamaican Mice,
YO!
Dem a ware dem sunglasses,
See how dem run,
And watch mi trial and crosses.

Dem all eat out di farmer rice,
Who get upset adi farmer's wife,
Farmer get chicken wid out him riiiiiiice.

Him never have no choice,
Him never get no riiiiiiiice.
Him never get no riiiiiiiiiiiiiiiiice.

Note: Dem = Them] Di = the] Mi = My] Adi = it's the]
Trial and crosses = Troubles] Wid = with]

A DOOR HINGE

A young man once came to fix a door hinge.
He was dressed to impress in a suit of orange.
Hammered his thumb and began to cringe.
His face was shade of a deep red tinge.

Then around like mad he ran in a circle.
Until his clothes had turned to purple.

GEORGIE PUDDING

To join in
{Children can shout out the highlighted words}

Georgie Porgy never got no,
PUDDING!
Out in your playground too busy,
PLAYING!
When the bells went
TING A LING A LING!
I said when the bells went,
TING A LING A LING!
I said when the bells went,
TING A LING A LING!
Georgie Porgy was,
THE LAST ONE IN!

HA CALLING JAMAICA QUICK!

Bring bring di phone a ring,
A long distance ting, hear di bring.
Bring bring adi sound of di ting.
Bring bring cuz come in.

"Yes Bless"
"Whappen cuz"
Tell mi what a gwarn?
Yu say yu jus cum off di road,
An yu just dun pick di corn.
How's you di family and how iz pappy Dee?
Yu say everybody criss and pappy Dee him garn a sea.

And how is Miss Mona she still have di shop?
What yu say fi hold up as yu soon come back.

She just a say howdy and wen yu cumin down?
"Just tell ar; soon as mi capture some English pound".

"Mi long overdue fi come down a yard
But credit kinda mash up and tingz kinda hard
Tingz always tuff fi ring back a yard
Fi ring back home we afi draw bad card
And fi keep in touch it seem like fraud".

See di card just dun again;
OH MY LARRRD!

Note; Ha = I'm / I
Afi = Have to/ Criss = Good./ Di = the/ Dun = Finish/
Fi = to/ Gwarn = Going on/ Iz = is/ Ar = her
Mi = me or I/ Tingz = Things/ Whappen = Hello/ Yu = you/
Larrrd = Lord

THE BIG SWISS CITY

I just came back from the big Swiss city,
The big Swiss city is Mighty Pretty,
Most of all in Geneva!

Trams, trains and automobiles,
Big snow tyres for most car wheels.
French, Italian all square meals.
Spend Swiss francs and you get good deals.
Trains will rumble through the nights.
While the city is lit with neon lights.
There seems to be tons of snow,
Everybody pulls together and the Swiss just flow.

I just came back from the big Swiss city,
The big Swiss city is Mighty Pretty,
Most of all in Geneva!

An air of calm can be found,
As you walk round the city or old town.
Anytime you feel like taking a break.
You can have a meal right on the lake
A place of joy and peaceful pleasure,
To fit you like it's made to measure.
It's like a city of wonderful beautiful treasure.
The memories I'll hold forever and ever.

I just came back from the big Swiss city,
The big Swiss city is Mighty Pretty,

Most of all in Geneva!

RATTY THE RAT

Lived in Rattery.
And he also owned a big cheese factory.
That made the best delightful cheese.
That lingered in the evening breeze.
Magnificently tasty,
Incredibly vapour.
And super savoury.
A special recipe, made with ease.
Day and nightly he made his cheese.
So the homeless mice didn't become thieves.
He gave them jobs in his factory.
So they'd never live a life of misery.
No more poison or mouse traps.
They even sold their cheese to cats.
For his innovation he was knighted.
Sir Ratty the Rat was so delighted.

Sir Ratty the Rat.
Still lives in Rattery.
And now he's opening a big bread factory.

THE CAT

Theeeeee cat is in the kitchen, eating out the rice.
One grain, two grain,
Instead of catching mice.

The cat is in the kitchen, sleeping on the mat.
One snore, two snore,
Instead of catching rats.
The cat is in the house, playing in the hall.
Catch the cat and put him out before night falls.

The cat is at the door,
Purring outside the house.
Morning has come;
And he's finally caught a MOUSE!

*Note: Sing or read The Cat to the melody of Knees Up
Mother Brown.
And try making your own actions for each line.*

FIRST OR LAST BREAK

It's alwayz the best thing,
When the bell starts to sing,

Ting, ting, ting, ting a ling
Ting a ling.

Quickly disappear books, paper and pencil.
Sunlit silhouettes breathless and still.

Shuffle screech wood and metal start their move.
Clip clop, clip clop like the sound of lambs' hooves.
Clippity clop, clippity clop, children skipping in their shoes.

Sounds of all type silently begin to hype.
Miss, Goal! Let's go, don't! Hooray!

A whistle whistles sharper, sharper than a kettle.
Moving motions in slow motions slowly begin to settle.
Buttons, tops, cloaks, caps and coats all cum in from the
drizzle.

Then back to class looking sharp,
Like thorns round a thistle.

THE FOOTBALL MATCH

"Boyz and girlz ina football match,
Boyz wanna kick it and girlz wanna catch

Boyz wanna win it and girlz wanna chat,
Before the girlz score, the chickens will hatch".

Now the boyz all think how this is their patch.
Bobby pass to Peter, Peter pass to Max,
There he goes down the flank,
These are just the fax.

Flowing cross the yard,
And skating on the grass,
The girlz build army, so he decides to pass,
But he was flattened by a tackle from sturdy little lass.
Play on says the ref, that's a great tackle Cass.

Slowly the girlz begin to turn the battle,
Winning every header, crunching in the tackle,
Chloe passes to Charlotte, Charlotte passes to Jill.
Then Jack and Sam were mesmerised by a touch of skill.
She had left them in a tangle as she was really brill.

The boyz began to panic, the boyz began to sweat.
As Jill was bearing in on goal and running out of breath,
Twinkletoed still she flowed the ball at her feet.
Into the mud doing good the boys face defeat.

Then a trip a foul from Timothy,
Up shouts the ref a PENALTY!
A voice shouts out, JUS GIVE IT TO ME!
I've got the skill and the ability.

The boyz are shell-shocked and hope she'll miss!
But up steps Lucy to deal with this.
Becky says go on girl you know you can do it.
So Lucy stepped to the ball and put her foot through it.

The event all happened in slow motion
Above all the din and the come a motion.
The shot was struck with perfection.
With the keeper in the mud stood to attention.
Goooooal!
One nil to the girlz I surely must mention.
And a red card for Timmy that's a suspension.
Boyz and girlz in a soccer game,
If the boyz lose they will feel so shame,
In the school yard or on the back lane,
Still one nil to the girlz and here comes the rain.

The boyz huffed and puffed and they tried in vain.

Shots from the yard landed on the main.
And shots from the lane ended up with pain.
And now they're upset,
As it's the end of their game
Hi fives from the girls as they shout we reign.
Singing after summer hols you can play us again.

"Boyz and girlz ina football match,
Boyz wanna kick it and girlz wanna catch".

THE PLAYGROUND AND ME

It's all about the playground, the one who really cares,
It's all about the playground forever standing there.

It's all about the playground; I can see it from my chair,
It's all about the playground, peculiar and square.

It's all about the playground, my favourite spot,
It's cold in the winter, but in summer well hot.
Let's paint a face on the playground, a big smiley one,
Am sure it's always lonely when everyone has gone.

Hundreds of feet skipping over its face
From ear to ear and back again, lots of children race.

It's all about the playground with smiles and tears,
It's all about the playground with shouts and cheers.

It's all about the playground where rain drops fall,
It's all about the playground, I wish time would stall.

It's all about the playground, we're like best friends,
It's all about the playground, I'm sad when playtime ends.
I told the playground to meet me, in the playground.
At three-thirty after school, as I would hang around.

The playground and me had lots and loads of space.
And before I went home I gave the playground a chase.
I never ever caught him but we had a laugh.
Before I could catch my breath, it was four and twenty past.

I said I must go, I said I better run.
When I see you tomorrow, we'll have more fun.

It's all about the playground, the playground and me,
It's all about the playground where I can think free.

A SALAD?

Thank you for the lunch suggestion,
I may have something more than a salad,
It's something my stomach will undoubtedly question.
And probably begin to play a ballad.

The only meat I don't eat is pork.
And the odd looking grumble fish.
With a spoon or a knife and fork,
Placed around a china dish.

I have been called fussy about my food.
When deciding what next to eat.
But food you know can be awfully rude.
And lift you off your seat.

And if it's not that you belch it out,
And cover your mouth with embarrassment.
I think that may have been the trout;
Now the air is full of its testament.

TODAY'S THE DAY

I captured the sky.
I, me, myself yes I.
I've captured spiders eating a fly,
And captured ants as they pass by,
Even roaming goats, cattle and sheep,
And captured an elephant falling asleep,
Captured a worm, captured a mouse.
The one that used to eat out the house,
I've captured a whale, a hyena.
Fast as they be I caught a cheetah.
Captured buffalo and even birds,
On this page I've captured wordz.
Through the lenz of my eye,
There you see I captured the sky.
I wonder what things you might capture.
The next time you decide to;
Use a camera.

TUG A WAR

It's a big tug a war with my mum.
And all day long we're having fun.
I will tug and she will pull.
I only win when my mouth is full.

It's a tug a war with my mum.
A big tug a war over my little thumb.

WHEN YOU'RE STUCK

When you're stuck for a rhyme,
And you can't find a line,
When your mind's not yours,
And it's very hard to find.
Don't send for Spider-man, Robin or Batman
Who you gonna send for?
Rappaman!

When you're feeling down,
And your face is on the ground.
Like you've just found a penny,
When you've lost five pound,
Don't send for Superman, Batman or Sand-man.
Who you gonna send for?
Rappaman!

So when life seems strange,
And you really need a change.
Just be honest with yourself,
Never tell yourself a lie.
Don't floss over the truth,
As the truth shall never die,
Don't send for Spider-man, Robin or Hentch man.
Who you gonna send for?
Rappaman!

So now you know just what to do, to make your dreams all
come true.
And let your choice of decisions be called intellect.
It's what you possess so you can make the first step.

Remember always try to be on top of your game.
And be the first to admit when your work is lame.
It's not a diss to miss and you know it's not a shame
If you learn from mistakes, you can still find your fame.

So don't send for Bad man, just be honest to yourself
As Badness is Madness and bad for your health.
So if you're really not sure and don't overstand.
Who you gonna send for?

RAPPAMAN!

Note: Overstand is Rastafarian terminology for to stand over, not under the things you have learned.

WITH PRECISION

Literally literacy competition,
Can you write a composition?
Literally literally literacy,
Have some fun and rhyme like me.
With rhyming, timing in precision.
And heart and mind are on a mission.
Wordz of iron and people listen,
Sparkle like fire and begin to glisten.
Every word spoke became a written
Style and thought of your decision.
The composition is literacy,
With a hint and dash of numeracy.
Alternatively between the lines,
Additions, subtractions an plus sometimes.
With yards, squares and rectangles,
And don't forget all the right angles.
Watch pen to paper make an incision.
And emancipate words from your prism.
Then handle your pen with precise precision,
And let the words on the page be your decision.

Note: *A prism is a transparent block used to*
disperse light into a spectrum

ALL ABOARD EXPRESS SEVEN

Express impress and be yourself.
Express impress and be yourself.
Ex-press train is here,
All year six yo come on draw near.
All aboard for level seven,
Only if you're ten and going on eleven.
Sit down yo steady and just be kool.
Places for all next stop new Skool.

Now Junior Skool's over and done,
We've got to be moving on.
In the blink of an eye before you know it,
Year six will all be gone.

Finding new places making new friends
Seeing new faces, while making new trends.

So all aboard ready to go.
Put away your doubts, move with the flow.
Don't get worried don't get scared.
Wherever there's a problem,
There's someone who cares.
So whenever you're down and feeling low.
Express yourself and let the pen flow.
Or express yourself to a friend
They'll make things better in the end.

There's gonna be ups and downs there always is.
Just express yourself politely,
And get on with the bizz.

We're steady approaching our new Skool.
Year seven to eleven it's gonna be just kool.

MY FIRST DAY

Oh my gosh-ness,
My first day at Skool.
I don't know how to get there,
I don't know what to do.

I'm watching my breakfasts and eating the telly.
There are dragonflies thoroughly deep in my belly.

I'm getting quiet worried now not long to go.
Hear the clock tick tock, helps time go slow.

Mum yells you're gonna be late!
Dad shouts put on your skates!
Tie up your socks and pull up lace.
It's sixty paces to the Skool gates.

Oh my gosh-ness I can't believe my eyes,
Everybody's so tall everything's so high.

And everything's strange and I feel so passive.
And I'm so small and everything's massive,
Must report to the hall via stairs or passage.
I stumbled on the boiler room I feel like a cabbage.

Oh my gosh-ness
My first day at Skool.
I can't find the hall and I feel like a fool.

Ding a ling a ling, was that the fire bell?
The boiler room is where am lost
It's getting hot as well.

Ding a ling a ling,
And are they even aware?
When the boiler door opened
My dad was shaving his hair.

As the ding a ling disappeared the clock hit the chair.
OH MY GOSH-NESS!
Was that a fright-mare?

YO RAY AND ME

Yo! Some bread or call it cash.
Raymond's a good friend of mine.
Me! Rappaman; I like to Rap.
Far reminds me of my town.
So the show it must go on.
La if you want to sing a song
T is in my poeTry
That will bring uz back to,
YO, YO, YO, YO.

Ray and me, me far so,
La Tee tee,
So just flow.
Wheeeeeen,
You you, know, the the,
Rhymes,
To to sing, sing sing.
You, Can, Rhyme, Most, Anything!

Note: Now try making and singing your own Yo Ray Me

WATA SUMTING!

Excuse mi please and tank yu,
Simple fi seh simple fi do.

Manners wi carry yu far,
Discipline and risspek,

Mi sure everybody know,
But act like dem forget.

Watch yu manners mind yu mouth,
Pinckney fi kool,
When elders deh bout.

Dem ya yout now a day's not a discipline.
Wat a sumting,
Mi seh wat a sumting,

Dem ya yout now a day's not a discipline.
Wat a sumting,
Mi seh wat a sumting,

Dem have ears ina dem head but not listening.
Eyes ina dem face and dem nar see a ting.
Never live a life,
But know everyting.
And try a act like Queen
An a act like king.

Wat A SUMTING,
Mi seh,
Wat A SUMTING!

Dem already dun know every likkle ting.
Wi can't tell dem not a one sumting.
So wi just seh time will tell and a hope you listening.
And yu never go a school fi duh di time wasting.

*Note: Fi = To} Wi = we/Will} Mi = I} Dem = Them}
Deh = are} Ya = here} Wat = what}
Sumting = Something} Ina = in their} Nar = not}
Nutting = Nothing} Seh = Say} Pinckney = children}
A ting = Thing/anything} Dun Know = conformation}
Duh = do} Di = the}*

Jamaican proverb: If yu nuh hear, yu wi feel.
If you don't listen then it might be hard times ahead

BOOKS FOR AFRICA

Char char trust for Africa,
Don't let books catch dust for Africa.
Char char trust a charity.
So kidz can read in Malawi.

It all started in two thousand and seven.
To remember two people who've now gone to heaven.
Charlotte and Veronica,
Were killed by elephants in Africa.
A tragic accident and tragic fate.
They'll always be remembered on this date.
Charlotte used to love to read.
And she saw Malawi children in need.
No libraries books or even paper,
So she would read her books and hand them over.
To Malawi Schools' boys and girlz,
So their eyes would begin to see new worldz.

Char char trust for Africa,
Don't let books catch dust for Africa.
Char char trust a charity.
So kidz can read in Malawi.
So today's a day where you can help,
Collect those books on a dusty shelf.
And turn them into knowledge and health.
Charity's about sharing your wealth.
Your old books are African new,
They're not so wasteful like me and you.
Even books can be recycled,
For Malawi children who should be entitled.

Char char trust for Africa,
Don't let books catch dust for Africa.
Char char trust a charity.
So kidz can read in Malawi.

Welcome To The

RISSPEK
APARTMENT

*Where you'll always remember to show nuff respect
and courtesy...*

BECAUSE WE CARE

Report it to sort it,
And we will support it.
Report it to sort it and we will be there.

Everyone needs support and T.L.C,
The thug, the mug and people like me.
The helpless, the lonely all need a friend.
To chillax and max with days on end.
No fakers, takers or heart breakers.
Peace and love will always mate us.
War and crime will only break us.
But real friendship will forever make us.

Report it to sort it,
And we will support it.
Report it to sort it and we will be there.

If you've been physically hurt sometime,
Or put in a distressed state of mind.
If you're pushed and you've been shoved.
And days have felt like there is no love.
Life feels drab washing down a drain,
As no one seems to see your pain,
Put these words on your brain.
And repeat them over again and again.

Report it to sort it,
And we will support it.
Report it to sort it and we will be there.

B to the U to the L.L.Y,
It's time to give someone a blye.
Which simply means don't make them cry.
And why not try just to be nice,

It's the only way to be cool as ice.
No means once, it don't mean twice.

And everyone knows you could be great,
But it's always the victims left in a state.
Report it to sort it and we will support it.
Report it to sort it and we will be there.
Report it to sort it because we care.

*Note: Jamaican proverb Duppy know who fi frighten =
ghost / bullies never pick on someone their own size}*

BORN WITH RISSPEK

You're born with risspek.
But you can lose it.
It's all up to you,
If you want to abuse it,
You're born with risspek,
And that's the real deal,
But it can be easily lost, if you start become too unreal.
Like especially if you start to lie, bully or steal.
Preserve risspek by keeping it real.

You're born with risspek,
You innocently earned it.
But it's all up to you,
To constantly preserve it.
A day shouldn't pass,
Where you haven't observed it,
Or even pass where you haven't served it.

You're born with risspek,
And you deserve it.
So this small blessing,
We have to preserve it.

But if you choose to abuse and lose it,
It's harder to resume the act to use it.

So the true facts of risspek,
I beg you please learn it.
And on your heart is where you wear it.

You're certainly all born with nuff risspek.
All I ask from you;
Is please let it reflect.

BLESS OUR HOME

BLESS THIS HOME
O LORD OF HOSTS.
HERE IN JAMAICA SWEET
ALONG THE NORTH COAST.

THIS HOUSE IS BLESSED

BY ANGELS ON EARTH,

AND WATCHED BY THEM ABOVE.

I DON'T WANT THIS PRAYER

TO BECOME A CURSE,
BY THOSE WHO SHOW NO LOVE.

KEEP ALL THOSE WHO ARE INVITED
SAFE FROM ALL HARM,
KEEP THEM SECURE O LORD,

WITHIN THY MIGHTY PALM.

O LORD KEEP WATCH THROUGH THE STARRY NIGHT,
AS WE WATCH FOR YOU IN THE MORNING LIGHT.
BLESS THIS HOME
O LORD OF HOSTS.
HERE IN SWEET JAMAICA'S COOL BREEZE
ON THE COAST.

CONSIDER YOUR LITTER

You **don't** have to be smart **to** find the right place.
Put rubbish in a bin **never** mek it escape.
Litter is the enemy binz likes to taste.
So pick up ya litter stuff it ina binz face.

Remember we're the guardians,
Of Mother Earth.
That's made from wood water sand,
And tons of dirt.
Don't throw away litter,
To make the dirt worse.
It'll be **up** to our necks,
In a couple a years.

Imagine a world all full of litter.
Walking to Skool wid paper mache in the gutter.
Or sliding round the hall in dirty tubs of butter.
And sticking to the floors on your rubbish and the clutter.

There would be lots of sickness, lots of disease.
The world would smell like a mouldy old cheese.
Everything would die: birds, bees and trees.
So put ya litter in a bin am asking ya please.

Cans, packets, bottlez of pop.
Everything that's sold ina shop.
Let's fill binz right up to the top.
And stick them at the gate for the garbage cop.

Everywhere we go humans don't consider,
The problems they cause,
When they're careless with,   l   itt   er...

Note: Please check the letters in bold to find a hidden message

FROM ENGLAND WITH LOVE

A light of hope and unity,
From year 8 to the nursery.
A place where you can go and see,
An International School of harmony.

The head, the staff and pupils,
All work together and share their skills.
Where children live like sisters and brothers.
And show respect to teachers and mothers.
Dads are cool and get involved,
Working together all problems solved.
A sight to behold a jewel of a School.

Where cultural conflict don't seem to exist.
Schools in the UK need to check out this,
And prioritise it at the top of their list.
Good cultural cohesion that must be bliss.

{Dedicated to the Staff and pupils of the International
School of Moscow}

NATURAL MUZIK

I can walk and walk and walk for hours,
And see and smell beautiful flowers.
Clouds above and soaring birds,
It frees my mind to write these words.

Distant or near hear the muzik.
The robin sings loud also the blue tits.
Magpies twitter and the crows will crow.
Wood pigeons coo deep and low.
The wind will blow the wind section.
And the leaves begin to clap with appreciation.
Hear the percussion running through the streams.
The sun's light display casts light beams.
Try noting the sounds you hear today,
Like a grasshopper scratching along your way.
Nature's muzik is all around.
When last did you stop to listen its sounds?

I can walk and walk and walk for hours,
And see and smell beautiful flowers.
It frees my mind to write these words.
With clouds above of singing birds.

PLANTS OF LIFE

Planting, planting, planting life.
Plant sum seeds day or night,
Bulbs or seeds into the dirt,
Not too deep don't bruise don't hurt.

Water daily and watch um grow,
And from little small seeds,
Big TREES will flow.

Into the wind, sailing in the breeze,
From little seeds you get big leaves.

Plants, bushes and even flowers,
Mary tends them daily,
For lots of hours.

Bulbs and seeds into dirt
Decorate the countryside for all it's worth.

RAPPAMAN TO THE RESCUE

Rappaman to the rescue, real risspek,
These are the things you mustn't forget.
It's the same respect that you expect.
So use these skillz for the best effect.

Manners and trust bring real courtesy,
It's Real Respect in simplicity.
Please and thanks you must express.
And let this be your daily success.
I know some people don't care less.
But always try to present your best.

Rappaman to the rescue picking off fleas.
Don't be a bully some don't you tease.
Excuse me sorry thanks and please,
Try every day, to use all of these.
Well it's the same risspek that you expect.
So use these words as they're correct.

Rappaman to the rescue get involved.
If you have to get a major problem solved.
And if you want to make things better for yourself,
Don't stack your problems all on a shelf.
Just talk it to sort it and we will deport it,
If you think you cannot manage it by yourself.

Rappaman to the rescue with a little advice.
If you hang out wid rats, you will get lice.
I should only say it once but I'm gonna tell you twice.
If you hang out wid rats there'll be trouble like rice.
Rappaman to the rescue put away your doubts.
Now's your chance to be risspek scouts.
Put it in your hearts then spread it all about.
Rappaman to the rescue over and out!

Note: www.fearless.org the voice of the youth, they can
help resolve the truth.

THE LAST ROSE

Roses are in many colours
When they can be found,

But the rarest of roses,
Are forever Brown.

If you possess such a rose.
Its price is priceless so I've been told.

If you ever see one weep,
It's just the way its little heart beats.

Welcome To The

THINKING
APARTMENT

Where you have lots of time to clear your mind and make great decisions...

THE WORLD

USED TO BE A BEAUTIFUL
AND ENCHANTED PLACE,

WHEN LOOKED AFTER
BY THE GRACIOUS GARDENERS,

THE GARDENERS
IN A BLINK;
WHO SEEM TO HAVE ALL BECOME
EXTINCT.

SO NOW SHE DIES HERE SHE LIES.
DO YOU SEE AND SMELL THE STINK?

*Note: Then how much can we waste,
Before we waste The Human Race?*

THE Ant and THE SKY

To the ant:

The sky probably starts at my knee.
But I don't know for sure how far they see.

Just legs dangling wherever they roam.
I suppose it would be like trying to walk through a comb.

Where does the sky stop?
More so where does it start?

And how do we preserve the sky?
It can't be replaced like an eye.
Therefore with no sky, there would be no ant,
Or even I.

I'M JUST A POEM

I'm just a poem but I am alive.
I'm just a poem I will always survive.
I have emotions, feelings, meanings and notions.
To the ink, the pen and the pad, I show my devotion.

I'm just a poem and I speak to you.
I see you and it's me you see.
I stare at you and you read me.
I am a mirror a reflection of you,
The correction of you the connection to you,
I'm just a poem I was written for you.
To take some time to see the full view.

You and I are on the same page.
Stage, rage even age.
I'm also that poem.
To guide you when you're growing.
To keep you in the knowing.
In wind, rain, sandstorm and snowing.
When you feel down and weak I keep you going.
Remember me; I'm just a poem.

BIG CITY LIGHTS

Moonlight dreams and big city lights.
Captivate the youth at night.

Shop front crews,
Fill avenues,
Watch out fidi fight!

Littered words,
No sense proverbs.

Broken promise,
Stone, bokkle and fist.

Designer wear tear,
Some get scare,
And run from di city light.

Lock down patrol,
Tek nuff soul;
Still, some never see di light.

Fren report,
Son get caught,
Caught up in a big city light.

Blue machine,
Come fi clean,
You give dem wages tonight.
Sight.
Seems like life you nuh like,
A who yu spite?

Maybe time fi do, fi who an who?
Nuh more big city light.

Down in certain cell,
Dark nuh hell,
Every shadow a pitch fi a fight!

So remember sumting,
Just have discipline,
Mek sure yu future bright!
Trouble will stir, problems occur;
If you nuh walk;

In a di light,

Right!

....

Note: Fidi = for the} Di = the} Sumting = something}
Tek = Take} Fi = To} Nuh = don't / No} Yu = you / your}
Mek = Make}

Jamaican proverb: When cockroach dem a keep party, im nuh invite fowl. = Be careful of the company you keep.
{Show me your company and I'll tell you who you are}

ANGELS

I see Angels.
At ground zero,
Of the sky,

Could I be an Angel?
That I can't deny.

What is an Angel?
Could it be
Someone like,

I?

SOUNDS OF SILENCE

Just me and the spirits;

Or is it me and my mind,
And the reality I find?

As the clock ticks down,
There's vibes all around,
To be found; hear the sound.

The silent voices in the depth,
Of silence;
I'm their antenna to the world.

I hear violent noises in the bowels of violence.
I must tell the world.

Blank paper a pen begins to write.
I diligently wait;
A messenger arrives.
I ask no questions, I follow the guide.
And take down each detail,
Each step, each stride.

The patient sound,
In the calm of patience.

The pen writes the words.

I'm their transmitter to the world.

To those that hear,
And see these things.

There is peace, joy and a guiding wind.

As I write down

What the Angels sing.

ASSURANCE

We all fear differences in our own individual way.
This surely inevitably will hinder us in our every day.
These are areas we need to improve.
To assure hate incidents are swiftly removed.

Ignorance of mind will make people perceive,
To their children they guide but truly mislead.
Even social society they try to deceive.
Simply because of what they believe,

So even aggressors need education and help,
They should ring H.I.R. Centres,
They need to ring it for themselves.

I hope this is a national campaign.
Victims all over,
Should never be put through such pain,

Don't suffer in melancholy, stagnant in silence.
There's a place to report all types of social violence.
Please don't stand by or tolerate,
Simply because it's not in your face,
United together we can reduce,
The harassment and displeasure of racial abuse,
Needing lots of help to change people's views,
To give people hope or life they never knew,

Whether violence is domestic or homophobic,
Show it a red card
And please report it.

We all fear differences in our own individual way.
This surely inevitably will hinder us in our every day.
These are areas we need to improve.
To assure hate incidents are swiftly removed.

Note: H.I. R = Hate incident reporting centres.

CAUGHT IN THOUGHT

Tell me what you really see,
When you look at someone like me.

Did you make the truth distort?
Are you captured in your thought?
Did you think of me az a colour?
Or simply az your east western brother?

Tell me what you really see,
When you look at someone like me.

Did you make the truth distort?
Are you captured in your thought?
Did you think about me as disable?
Well I'm always willing and I'm able.

Tell me what you really see,
When you look at someone like me.

Did you make the truth distort?
Are you captured in your thought?
Did you think of me as ugly?
If you'd open your eyes you'd see my beauty.
And then you would get to truly know me.

Tell me what you really see,
When you look at someone like me.

Did you make the truth distort?
Are you captured in your thought?
Am I the book you've never read?
Or am I all the things that you've said?

Tell me what you really see,
When you look at someone like me.

Then tell me what you would do,
If someone thought these things of you.

*Note: Beauty is in the eye of the beholder or the owner
And experience teaches wisdom}
Wisdom brings knowledge and overstanding
Never judge a voice by how it sounds on the phone.
But you can judge a tree by its fruits.*

FACES PLACES

Faces places in different spaces.
Faces places in different times.

Illusion of time to blow your mind.
I've seen it through the windows of mine eyes.
Lonely faces places and desert wastes.
Still there seems to be a lot of hungry faces.
The future hastes all type of traces.
That's why we can't stop, for no time wasters.

Asteroid places with money faces.
Billions of dollars gone into spaces.
Galactic faces all type of traces.
But the fight goes on a couple of paces.
Extraordinary cases loose like your laces.
Still they want to lock down a lot of aces
No more embraces from friendly faces
As time goes by no family traces.

Dishonour, disrespect and nuff disgraces.
Be on guard, aware and in a your bases.
The future hastes all types of tastes
That's why we can't stop for no time wasters.
So let life embrace us to fill empty places
Try to understand different faces.
Don't lose your places in a rage of races.
Or somebody else will be taking your places.

Faces places in different spaces.
Faces places in a different times.

Note: There are many different and similar nations
in the world.

But there is only **One Human Race.** It comes in a wide variety of different styles and colours. Like eyes, hair, shoes and socks, shirts, skirts and even your jumpers. Life is a great and humble blessing which we all share and have in common.
And as Humans we do all we can do to preserve it.
We are one of the softest tissues on the planet and need food, clothes and shelter to survive.

OH MAMA EARTH

The Earth is CRYIN
Who will dry her TEARS?

The EARTH is DYIN
Who are her PEERS?

Who is her family or next of kin?

The EARTH is trEmBLIng
Does anyone know her FEARS?

The EARTH is suffering From Internal CANCER.
Is there a doctor in the house to give uz an ANSWER?

We will all miss the EARTH one day,
For the neglect we've shown we'll all have to pay.

Unless we start to CHANGE our WAYS,
And make it better for the rest of our days.

The EARTH is sick
We must all do something to SAVE it.
The EARTH is our HOME,
As Home is Earth.

This is all we've known from our childbirth.
Don't let it die of this terrible thirst.

LET'S CALL A DOCTOR, TEACHER OR NURSE.

TO PUT THIS PROBLEM IN
E S R E V E R.

MANNAZ AND RISSPEK!

Manners were born before risspek.
Honour came to keep them in check.
When manners and risspek both fell out.

Honour was there in our hour of doubt.

Your word is your honour,
So be true to your word.

It's only yourself you will defeat.
If to yourself and others you show deceit.

Note: Mannaz = Manners} Risspek = respect

CAN I HAVE

Can I have your name?
Can I have your game?
Can I have your fame?
Can I have your chain?
Can I have your pen?
Can I have your paper?
Can I have your stapler?
Can I have it later?
Can I have your book?
Can I have a look?
Can I have; what was it now?

"Then let me tell you before you sneeze
You might just get all of these
I can also give you Q's and P's
If I can have a simple"
PLEASE!

ONE MORE NOTE

I've taken note with stamp and letter.
What can be done to make Britain feel better?
I've seen how long she's been under the weather.
But still she seems to be getting much wetter.

What can be done for Britain to be great?
And I don't mean pillage, destroy and rape.
Nor do I mean a new debate.
Quality equality before it's too late.
That's all we need for Britain to be GREAT!

BLACK AND WHITE

{Trilogy to Pen Marries blank paper and the Honeymoon}

The pen and the paper were now truly married.
Too long a time apart they had tarried.
Said the paper to the handsome pen,
I'll love you till the very end.
You're the only one who thought of me as a friend.

Said pen to the paper we were meant for each other.
I am black you are white,
Look at the way we can unite.
But it seems that aliens still want to fight.

Look how you bring out the best in me,
And I bring out the best in you.
Without you there is no we,
Without me there is no you.

Remember the days when we were divided,
And I could never be with you.
Every day I was truly down-hearted.
Every day was the colour of a deeper blue.

Said paper to the pen we need children,
Our words are not for the few.
Let's spread the words just like seeds,
And hope and pray they turn to big trees.

Deep roots, strong branches and big broad leaves.

Years from now we'll forever be,
People will look, they'll read and see.
How the pen and the paper had set them free.

Welcome To the

SHORT STORY APARTMENT

Between the lines for a ready steady read indeed...

THE LAST BOOK I READ

How do you bring a book to life?
Take one home and read tonight.
I've read books and done reviews.
Now check this to spot some clues.

The last book I read I was swallowed by a **whale,**
If you know the book then you should know the tale.
The last book I read where I sailed upon the sea,
With a **parrot** on my shoulder which book could it be?

The last book read there were **snakes** on her head,
Did I tell you the title? I know I never said.
The last book read I put a **cloak** around my jotter.
Then it disappeared like the cloak of have I got ya?

The last book I read, started with **a shed,**
And then to my new school where I was swiftly led.
Now all over schools this book has now spread.

The last book I read it stared me in the eyes,
I had to put it down as I was nearly **hypnotised.**
It was all in my head is what I realised.
Did you catch the clue, are you sharp and are you wise?

The last book I read I was stalked by a crock.
Then I ran for my life, when I heard the **tick tock,**
Was it a crock or big alligator?
I'm not really sure; when I said see you later.

The last book I read is where I met an ice Queen,
She turned the land to **snow** when it should have
looked green
If you know the Queen you will know which book I mean.

The last book I read had my own **apartment**.
And in another room it made me feel confident!

The last book I read fell asleep on my knee,
And then came the moment I could certainly see.
I'd love to read a story written by DC
But if you get a chance write one b4 me.

{Answers to the **9** mystery books in bold
from **Whale** to **Apartment**, here's a clue.
It's behind you. Or try at the back of this book.
If you have to really take a look.

I'M BOOORED!

A boy once said, well mummy I'm booored!
So she gave him a job he simply adored.
The task to send his mind abroad.
To find some words to rhyme with snored.

She never thought he'd do what she'd said.
So off to his room to lie on his bed.
Then all these words poured from his head.
While some were stored in the pencil lead.

Words can be upset when being ignored.
In your head and on paper they can be stored.
I remember the time 3 lions roared.
The day we won and I even scored.
The day before I went abroad.
On a jumbo jet,
All aboard!

Sun, sand, sea with a slick surf board.
But remember last holiday, it simply down poured.
The day which I tried to win an award,
And tackled a fish with a mouth like a sword.
Mum began to scream!
Dad began to applaud.
But I still ended up on a hospital ward.
I've only been scratched; I haven't been gnawed

With mum sobbing, crying and praying to the lord,
My little Billy brother just hawked and snored.
Save my big brother, my sister implored.
My dad said son; you'll be soon restored.

The doctor was a mechanic who drove a rusty Ford.
And on his wages that's all he could afford.
He'd done time in jail and been called a fraud.
And been a one-man band, but only played a harpsichord.
Also the house where he lived was made of cardboard.
While he had to pay rent to his stingy landlord.

I thought he was going a bit overboard.
When he tried to stitch my umbilical cord.
I only came for a scratch, here on mi headboard
So up went a knuckle and he was floored.
Never again will I feel bored.
And if I do, it's my own accord.

THE LOST WORD

Today's the day the search began,
Amongst the grass and trees,
Even a frantic search today took place,
Throughout the A, B, Cs.
Worried Scholars and Activists,
Paparazzi scouts, Journalists,
Columnists and Wordsmiths,
Scientists and Psychologists.
MPs and Nationalists.
Has all that we've done now come to this?
And disappearing away to a word of mist.

What's the problem, haven't you heard?
It seems we've definitely neglected a word.
For sure words have been lost before,
But what can replace what this stood for?
Was it stolen and is no more?
Or did it run though the open door?
I dare not shall not will not say,
Which word we may have lost today.

It's been abused being hardly used.
And has wandered off and felt confused.
It's a sad sad way for this to end,
I jest you not and don't pretend.
And hope you're not the one to blame,
And bound this word in a rusty chain,
Flushed down the toilet rinsed down the drain,
It's a crying sorrow and a real pain.
We may never use this word again.

Do you know where this word could **be?**
If you do please set it free.
Or if you find or come **a**crostic.
Tell everyone we haven't lost it.
Start to help, seek and find,
Or it may be the fall of mankind.
Research your words and vocabulary.
Reassert this word to the dictionary.
You know it wi**ll** bring back sincerity.

Today's the day the search began,
Amongst the grass and trees,
Even a frantic search today **t**ook place
Throughout the A, B, Cs.
Worried **S**cholars and **A**ctivists,
Paparazzi scouts and **J**ournalists.
Columnists and **W**ordsmiths,
Scientists and **P**sychologists,
Has all that we've done now come to this?
And disappearing away to a word we'll miss.

Note: Do you know where this lost word could be?
The word is hidden within this mystery poem.
Did you manage to find it?
If not I'm sorry but it is there, have another look. Try
*looking at the letters in **bold**. They will spell a word.*
Some letters have been left plain in the missing word.
And some letters are just bold for fun.
Read and seek an good to go!

ANOTHER TALE

Dick Turpin

{Adapted from The Highwayman by Alfred Noyes}

A silver liquid on trickling stream, at time invisible to trace,
On silent roads and idle paths, the moon shows its face.
I hearken to Bess, a sound I hear it's time for me to race.

Nighttime falls upon the heath downcasts a changing light.
The murky air arising takes off in upward flight.

With leather clad around my back, I fear the night I don't
feel that.
The time has come to take the lead,
And dive right into the eye of the breeze.

Giddy-up giddy-up giddy-up, mustn't break stride.
Giddy-up giddy-up giddy-up, over fallen trees I glide

A fragment of a picture like a view on distant sea,
An abstract figure of moon-shade, I pass between the
trees.

To the landlord's black-eyed daughter,
Her lips a cherry wine,
The landlord's black-eyed daughter is a lady friend of mine.
Past patrols and horses' men, the stealth to elude.
With companion to dim-lit ground,
Nobody must intrude.

I hope she decides, this hurts my sides,
I pray she will elope
Too many times I've taken this chance, I fear the
hangman's rope.

80

By the old barn I passed and overheard,
While stealing a sack of oats,
The ostler's vexation, hell, damnation as he sent for the
redcoats.

With no time to delay, I must make hay,
And hastened to sound the alarm,
But when I saw the landlord's daughter,
The landlord's black-eyed daughter, I melted at the stroke
of her arms.

I was short of speech, so stamped my feet,
And pointed to the gates,
I must take lead, I pray take leave,
And dive back into the eye of the breeze.
With her long black hair sailing, breached o'er
Shoulder Bridge.
Her big black reflecting eyes, lash behind her lids.
The air was filled with sweet scent, freshly dancing
in the wind.
Ah, it so reminds me of sweet tonic, honeys and gin.

I bid make haste to my sincere, tight grip to my back.
As muskets bade before me,
Directed at my path,

Giddy-up giddy-up giddy-up, mustn't break stride.
Giddy-up giddy-up giddy-up, into muskets raised high.

A flash of musket fire! Cascades death like a moonlit flare.
Hot coals of burning thunderbolts pass through me
like cold air.

I felt a grasp loose from round my back!
The extra weight I no longer bared.
As I dashed to cross rickety bridge, we fell to their snare.

A lift of neck; a tilt of head, a purse of gold
had turned to red.
Fallen mask from a pain-filled face;
Smears of blood decorated lace.

And the landlord's black-eyed daughter
Was foiled to escape.
I felt her heart pound beneath as I tried to arise.
But the source of energy had flowed from me as we stared
death
In each other's eyes.

She reached for a golden pistol strapped to a velvet leg.
Before the guards upon us fall,
I know we'll surely be dead.

With weakened finger and from steady aim,
Her body fell to limp and ceased from inward pain.
Before I go, I also know, we'll all be together again.

As in life, so in death forever shall we be.
Our spilt blood entwined,
Between us you find, it will flow right back to the sea.

As all rivers flow, as you know, to the ocean where they are
free.
And on nights when restless moonlight brings the mist over
land.
A horseman goes riding with woman at his hand.

A silver liquid on trickling stream, at times invisible to
trace,
On silent roads and idle paths, the moon shows its face.
I hearken to Bess! A sound I hear it's time for me to race.
Nighttime falls upon the heath downcasts a changing light.

The murky air arising takes off in upward flight,
A fragment of a picture, a view of distant sea,
An abstract figure of moon shade, we are between
the trees.

The air was filled with sweet scent, freshly dancing
in the wind.
Ah, it still reminds me of sweet tonic, honeys and gin.

Giddy-up giddy-up giddy-up, mustn't break stride,

Giddy-up giddy-up giddy-up,
Through eternity we glide.

Giddy-up giddy-up giddy-up,
Where peace and love abide,
The landlord's black-eyed daughter forever grips my sides.

*Note: This was written from the horse's view
of the situation.
See if you can spot where the horse has to be telling
this story.*

*There are many clear indications; you may find more.
Have fun discussing with your friends, group or class.
Also check the letters in **bold** to find a hidden message.*

TRAVELLING BACK

A man set off to find himself and found himself indeed.
Wooden planks, ropes and sheets,
Blown across the seas.

With associate men, to the world's end,
Never sure what they would find.
Days and night on tormented seas,
The opposites must collide.

Collide like magic as calm sets on high.
We need the opposites to survive.
So when travelling back to the opposite side,
I am sure that you will find.
All that you see don't despair,
It mustn't blow your mind.

A man set off to find himself and found himself indeed.
Wooden planks, ropes and sheets,
Blown across the seas.
As mass appeared on yonder line,
Men armed to teeth lest they die.

From other side whence they flowed,
He saw a man whose skin just glowed.
As far and wide from where I ride,
He's very similar to I.

Who are you he asked with pause in face;
I might have to destroy all your trace.

The man with the skin that glowed said;
As we all share this beautiful shelf,
To destroy me is to destroy yourself.

The man with the skin who seemed
To glow; was in no hurry to leave.
I was ready to take him down at once,
He must have a trick up his sleeve.

But what is my reason this man must die?
Because his shade is a little more golden than I.
As he gazed at me with a sparkling eye,
I bid to insist, how do you exist?
He offered me fruit and spoke of truth,
If this man dies, then so shall I.

So if I've reached some stage in life
And I don't want him around.
Then maybe I am in danger,
From my men who have me surround.

I've travelled from far you understand.
But now I see the man in man.
A colour's just a colour;
I see no colour in nature,
Where one feels it's much greater,

I now know a man just as a man.
And now I overstand.

A man set off to find himself and found himself indeed.
Wooden planks, ropes and sheets,
Then blown across the seas.

To the opposite side to the world's end,
Never sure what he would see.

To find himself and family.
People like you and me.

Then found his roots and branches,
Are apart of a global tree

Note: Overstand = Things I never knew before. When I
never knew or understood the problem, issue or subject.
Now I know, I stand over the problems, issues or subjects.
A Rastafarian terminology

....

If there was no light we would all look the same,
But as the sun rises above we all can show our shame.

ST MISCELLANEOUS
GRAMMAR SKOOL

Hi welcome to St Miscellaneous Grammar Skool
for Boyz and Girls.
As I show you around please take notes.
You can leave your bags here and hang up your coats.

Here are some names please try to remember,
Of the heads of departments and staff members.

The head of the Skool is Miss Gee Conduct,
You won't see her today with a little good luck.
Mismanage is the deputy head; she's late to skool,
an late to bed.

There are three secretaries, Misplace, Misprint
and Mislays.
They're always putting papers in the wrong drawers
or trays.

The Skool nurse is called Mishap.
In case of minor cuts, bust noses, runny colds,
And she even has a bed, where you can take a nap.

Quiet please on this corridor,
The library's a place you cannot talk.
By Misjudge and Mischance it is stalked.
They have ears like Elephants and eyes like a Hawk.
The head of art is Misappropriate,
We never make what we want to make.
She's also helped by Trendy Mistress.
I once saw her give the milkman a kiss,

Missal is head of the Skool's RE.
Misfit and Misfortune do the entire PE.
Miss it is the only one who teaches I.T.
And I think it's Miscarriage who does biology.

In maths it's Mistake and Misapprehend.
Miscast in drama where we like to pretend.
Misgiving teaches all the PHSE.
Misguided and Mistral share the Geography.

In History it's Misconception, Misadventure,
Misinform and Mislead.
If to detention you are sent, it's Misdemeanour,
Misdeeds, Mischief and Misspent.
The detention rosters set by Miscreant.

The muzik teacher is called Miscible.
The head dinner lady is called Miserable.
She runs the hall with an iron fist.
Her second in command is Misanthropist.
Now the English teachers have good intent.
Misunderstand, Misused and Misrepresent.

In Science we get up to all kind of tricks.
With Miscellany, Mischievous, and the other ones
called Miss.
Now am nearing the end of our staff register list.
Let me see, ah yes, there's a couple I've missed.

Our French teacher's French I have to mention.
Miss Mission is a lady with French connections.

The Skool gardener is called Mistletoe.
She keeps the grass green just like the hedgerows.

The Skool caretakers are never dull.
They go by the name of Mister and Miss trustful.
They always seem to make you smile.
Oh and their dog is called Missile.

The Skool governor is called Missing.
Whenever we need some extra funding.
Down the road from the Skool is where she lives.
She has a secretary called Missive.
I can't think of anyone I've dist.
So this is the end of our staff register list.

Note: most of the teachers' names are in the dictionary. See if you can find them and their meanings if you don't know what the word means. I think you will find that their names suit the subjects they teach or the jobs they do. What does missive mean? Ask a dictionary.

This poem can also be used as a memory game show. Divide the class or family into small groups of two to six groups. Then choose team names and captains as the captain is the only one who can give the answers after discussing with their team.

Someone neutral will have to read the poem and then ask the groups which teacher or who teaches which subjects or jobs they do. Ask the groups to keep their own score and keep a check on scores every so often.

Points of 10 to 50 can be awarded for each correct answer given. To be fair, each group has one attempt at answering the question. If the question is still up for grabs it can be offered again to the team that answered first. The reader must decide how many points they give per correct teacher. I suggest starting at 10 and after two to three rounds go to 20 or 25 points. Teams behind may need to catch up.

Example: Which teachers can be found teaching History? There are four teachers and four groups. Each group will have a chance to give a teacher's name. A group may pass and it can be offered to the next group in order. If there are only one or two teachers it will be first hand up or buzzer.

At the end, if they have struggled, ask the groups in the same order. Can they remember any of the teachers' names and subjects or where you will find them? Only the ones you haven't used for extra 10 to 20 points to build up their scores. Any group member may answer at this point. It can be fast and furious.

The winners are the team with the most points. The scorer will also have to remember names used. So I suggest making notes or you will find yourself giving points out for answers already given. This may cause unrest amongst the groups. Your word is final.

This is just for fun but you can decide on any prizes for the winners, maybe a day off!

I think not.

I'm sure you will have loads of fun hearing the English language at times being misused and nearly abused. Some contestants will create new names for teachers that don't exist. And a couple of teachers' names will be said and sound related but those teachers work at another school.

Or if it's only two of you, why not just test each other with say 10 questions each.

Who has the best memory in the class, group or family?

Last of all, this is a memory game and groups are not allowed to write when the poem is being read. You can let one person write. You decide, but read the poem swiftly to confuse them.

Have Fun!

Welcome To The

CULTURE
APARTMENT

To keep in touch with ways and traditions...

CULTURE IS

What does culture mean to you?
C is Customs to make you feel good with family and friends
like you know you should.
U is Unique in the things you do and the ways you greet, eat
and where you meet.
L is Language to help you debate and communicate.
Organises and set the date. This then would be;
your literacy.
T Traditions offer time together and things to do,
say and remember.
U = Universal and Unique to U mans.
R is Rules or Religion; it shouldn't be you who makes
all the decisions
E is for Education so you can simply build a nation.
This is what culture means to me. They're just some
of the things
That makes me
Meeee!

Note: Now try making your own list of things that make up
your culture.
And try looking at other cultures and make a list
Then see what you share with other cultures.
Please not in this book.
Find some paper to store your data.
To tell me later about your culture.
Nuff Risspek!

UNITED NATIONS IN COMMUNICATIONS

{Dedicated to the students at Cranford Community Ccollege}

Respect people and their languages,
Human beings are just like sandwiches.
Communication is simply the key.
To build a better community.

Salam means Hello in Turkey.
Please use these words and just feel free.
To say Thank You in Urdu.
These words are made for me and you.
Shocre is the word that we use.
To speak another language if we choose.
Sabai Dii Mai is Thai, for How Are You?
So respect one and all is what we should do

Education will take us all further.
From Pakistan to Poland or even Jamaica.

Sorry, Excuse Me, Thank You and Please.
Try saying these in Japanese.
Konichiwa means Hello in Japan.
While Thank You in Yemen just say Shukran.
Khuda Hafis to bless when respect is high
So learn another language and don't be shy.

Respect people and their languages,
Human beings are just like sandwiches.
Communication is simply the key.
To build a better community.

And don't fi-get wen yu in Jamaica
Likkle More means see you later.
Hail up, bless an wah gwarn.
Are simply greetings from dusk till dawn.
And just a reminder of how they're so polite
When dem pass yu in di evening,
Dem tell yu good night.

Respect people and their languages
Human beings are just like sandwiches.
Communication is simply the key
To build a better community.

*Note: Fi-get = Forget} Khuda hafis = muslim greeting}
Wen = When} Yu = You} Dem = They}*

HIS STORY or MY STORY

This is history, this is history, this is history,
this is his story.
This is
His Story.
His story says we were found when we were never lost.
His story says we're the labourers never the boss
His story says we are alien and different,
We had never given it a thought,
Only when been captured, caught, sold, tortured, butchered
or bought.

His story says we are inferior and see themselves
are superior.
His story says we are not to be trusted around their
children and wives.
His story says we will eat them without forks or knives.

His story says we are lazy and don't know how to keep time.
Organize a function or form a line.
His story says we are born to be servants and labourers.
So they divided rule and tried to conquer us.
His story says we are savages without languages
We only know of mummies and bandages.

His story says we are incapable of any form of civilization.
Never mind about their colonization.
Of our homelands and our wonderful nation
This is his story not my story.

My story started long before his story.
Their books and scholars have tried to ignore me.
My story is of ancient kemit and Nubian kingdoms.
They were beautiful magnificent cities, once in Africa's regions.

Wisdom grew from Timbuktu.
Ask the Greeks the Romans they all passed through.

Organized and centralized as a society,
With the world's first biggest library.
With scholars and students at its university.

Where love thy neighbour, a stranger was a priority,
And everybody was greeted, treated like family.
And every other day, some would say, please marry me.

Councils ordained fair trade with their neighbours.
People were paid commodities for their labours.
My story is of raw facts, artefacts, books of mysteries,
within its pages.
Showing how life should be lived and taken in stages.
My story is from a family point of view.
Talk to the elders, you'll always find something new.
We all should know there are two sides to a story,
Then you should all know why they choose to ignore me.

Pray tell me not; they still want our glory.

To destroy my story and even scorn mi
So if the truth should be known.
This is his story.

And his story;
Well his story
Is just like listening Jack a bore mi.

Note: All mathematical learning during the medieval period
was available to Timbuktu scholars: arithmetic, algebra,
geometry and trigonometry, during the great Islamic reigns
of the Mali Empire and the Songhai Empire.
Timbuktu was also known as the City of Books
Ref: http://www.cwo.com/~lucumi/timbuktu.html

African proverb: Until the lions have had their say the
hunter will have all the glory.

FATHER OF BLACK HISTORY

Who's the father of black history?
Now it's never gonna be a mystery.
Carter G Woodson is his name,
He put black scholars in the hall of fame.

He graduated at Harvard University.
Where he received an honorary PhD.
He studied Negro life and history.
About the Africans' contribution to society.
In 1926 founded Black History Week.
And gave black people all a chance to seek.
Black heros and sheros from the past.
And even today their works still last.
Mary Seacole, a Jamaican nurse,
By the British war office she was cursed.
She funded a trip from her very small purse,
To save wounded soldiers as they came first.

And Garrett Morgan your future's bright
You gave us all the traffic lights.
And Fredrick Douglas, who was a slave.
Who became a free man bold and brave.
He fought for justice and equality.
For you, me and everybody.
And even as time flies past.
Some books have been written and built to last
A French African, Alexander Dumas,
An author, a writer that's strictly class.
A round of applause or three cheers.
He's the one who wrote The Three Musketeers
And when his pen began to flow,
He wrote The Count of Monte Cristo.

Who's the father of black history?
Now it's never gonna be a mystery.
He put black scholars in the hall of fame.
Google www and just add their names.

....

Note: A couple of useful sites to help with Black History Month:
http://www.freemaninstitute.com/woodson.htm
http://inventors.about.com/od/blackinventors/a/black_inventors.htm

"A people without the knowledge of their past history, origin and culture is like a tree without roots", Rt Hon Marcus Garvey. On Education
"EDUCATION is the medium by which a people are prepared for the creation of their own particular civilization, and the advancement and glory of their own ethnicity".
http://www.africaresource.com/rasta/sesostris-the-great-the-egyptian-hercules/the-wise-teachings-of-marcus-garvey/

HOW?

How do we build a community?
With peace, love and harmony.
How do we build a better place
For our future families to be safe?

Everyone looking for purity.
Without risspek and courtesy.
Neglect doesn't build unity.
Just hate. destruction and poverty.

How do we build concrete trust?
It seems risspek has gone bankrupt.
Turned to rust and full of dust.
More severe has gone corrupt.

How do we build a community
With every nation in unity?
Isn't the world ours to share?
Why are we fighting for a square?
Think of things we share in common.
Like sleeping, breathing and eating salmon.
Curry dish, veg dish or even gammon.
And all of the choices we have to fathom.
Still some won't hear the voice of reason.
Inside their fort is their cohesion.
If common courtesy is your aim,
Then our objectives should be the same.

How do we build a community?
With peace love and harmony.
How do we build a better place
For our future families to be safe?

And Welcome To
YOUR
APARTMENT

Along with your very own personal door sign...

{ PRIVATE }

PLEASE KEEP OUT!
DO NOT DISTURB
THIS MEANS YOU

YOURSELF!

Wah Gwarn, Salamalaikum, Dzien Dobry, Howdy do!
I bring greetings and Risspek to all within my view.

Be yourself and no one else.
Whoever told you to be someone else?
Be yourself and no one else.
Whoever told you to be someone else?

The sun rises for you and everybody too.
The dew from heaven is 4 me and you.
We see the sky the same colours too.
Sometimes grey sometimes dark,
It's sometimes sunny and blue.

We breathe the same air you and me.
You like coffee I like? Drinking chocolate!
I see no reason to disagree,
And start a war with my army.

So!
Be yourself and no one else,
Whoever told you to be someone else?
Be yourself and no one else.
Whoever told you to be someone else?

The earth is a house 4 everyone 2 share.
I hope from today we all take care.
A house like ours is truly rare.
You'll never find another like this out there.
So always try to be sharp, smart, cool and aware.
Most of all, just please take care.
So be yourself and no one else!

Note: Wah gwarn = Jamaican greeting}
Salamalaikum = Islamic greeting meaning peace be upon you
Sat Sri Akal = Sikh greeting for God is True}
Dzien Dobry = Polish greeting for hello

ALPHABET RAP

This is my Alpha rap.
Looking forward, reflecting back.
My Alpha rap is all about me.
Just check out my A to Zee.

A = Ambitious
B = Brother
C = Compassionate
D = Determined
E = Eternal
F = Father
G = General
H = Helpful
I = Inquisitive
J = Journey
K= Keeper
L = Loving
M = Mother
N = Neatly
O = Oracle
P = Polite
Q = Query
R = Realistic
S = Sister
T = Traditions
U = Unique
V = Valiant
W = Wisdom
X = X-ray
Y = Yesterday
Z = Zeal

You can now try to write your own Alpha rap.
Using all the letters of the alphabet,
Just think of a word that represents you in a positive way.
And write them down just start today.
They'll guide your steps in all you do.
Trust me, it works as I trust you.

Note: I'm sure you can find more than one word for certain
letters.
I would suggest to you, use no more than three.
If this helps you to see,
Your personality.

BLANK PAGES

Life is all about levels and stages.
Some never seem to leave first bases.
Run around ignorant and act outrageous.
Never took some time to fill in the pages.

Everything in life has its places.
Everybody wants to be at the big-time races.
Some just wishing time pass by.
Can't really walk but still wanna fly.

Knowing everything especially about nothing.
Why race to grow old some still keep on wishing.
You should take a long time to get there.
It's like now you're here, tomorrow you're where?

Blank pages can become old rages.

Life is all about levels and stages.
Some never seem to leave first bases.
A postcode, a street full of ignorant faces.
No one knows about airs and graces.

And terrified to travel to different places.
A trail of destruction is their traces.
Then always on somebody else's cases.
All because they never filled in their pages.

Now they've become wandering teen strangers.
When they just should have been cool teenagers.

What we learn in school will help to shape us.
And what we don't know can even shame us.

So please make some time to fill in your pages.
As life you know should go on for ages.

So don't let your book be full of Blank
Spaces.

Note: Those who fail to prepare are only preparing to fail.
And it's not everything that glitters is gold.
You cannot plant rice and expect corn to grow

CAN YOU BE?

Can you be a better person?
Things left unchecked will only worsen.
Can you help someone else
And think of them as yourself?
Yo the world needs a helping hand.
So stand, grow tall and understand.
We all could do with a little more love.
Or even just a tiny hug.
To tell you the truth,
Honestly,
Honesty will set you free.
Hate is only a four-letter word.
So small but it can destroy our world.
Love is also a four-letter word,
For these four letters I'll be the shepherd.

Can you be a better person?
Things left unchecked will only worsen.
Can you be a better human?
Tomorrow you get to see a Newman.
How will you know what's real
When you won't allow yourself to feel?
Why not give yourself some time a chance
And give your soul some time to dance?
Do you assume or research the facts
Or follow the leader like wolves in packs?.
A maze for life with wrong decisions,
The right ones help you stay out of prisons.

So it goes we all make mistakes.
And everyone's looking for easy breaks.
So take some, make some time to reflect.
And decide what you want
To really do next.

Can you be a better person?
Things left unchecked will only worsen.
Can you be a better Newman?
Tomorrow you'll get to see a Human.

Note: *A Leopard cannot change its spots, but we can definitely change our ways.*

DECISION

Are you a wanna be
Or are you a gonna be?

Do you really wanna be
Just like a wanna be?

Or are you gonna really be,
Just like how you should be?

I suppose we'll have to wait and see.
Just who you're really gonna
B

Note: Wanna = Want to} gonna = going to
When the stars were created there was one designed for
each and every one of us.
All you have to do is reach out and claim yours.

DISTRACTIONS

A thought of mind with adverse reactions.
To lose focus on the main attractions.

A pause in time where nothing is clear.
I wonder if I were really here.

How long, how much have I been distracted?
And when I got back how I reacted.

Did I lose some time or was my knowledge inclined.
To be suitable for the thought I had in mind?

A second or two and I'm back on the plot.
But it seems the thought of mind I forgot.

Distractions, a mind breakdown
Of chain reactions.

Can we train our minds to truly focus
And centre our thoughts on the things before us?

Maybe distractions we have are a vision in time.
Because in distractions we lose or make time.

Maybe distractions are meant to be.
Part of time for fulfilment of prophecy.

So long as your objectives are still safe and secure.
Maybe for distractions there is no cure.

But continue forward to achieve your aim.
Understand your distractions as they're part of the game.

A nature of distraction in a physical sense
Was not necessarily of a physical intent.

But maybe for some reason,
You may have been sent.
Or that pause in time where nothing is clear,
I wonder if you were really here.

YOUR FOCUS

My Focus is my success.
That's why am gonna try my very best.
I'm gonna be all I can be.
Study hard at school and go UNIVERSITY!

Now say it again and mean it this time
Repeat every syllable, sentence and rhyme.
My Focus is my success.
That's why am gonna try my very best.
I'm gonna be all I can be.
Study hard at school and go UNIVERSITY!

Everybody wants cash, a husband or wife.
But I've got to stay focussed an map out mi life.
Don't be a nugget and why be a mule?
And all I hear some say is that I'm too cool for School.

So let me wish me all the best.
As I journey forward on my quest.
Repeat these wordz just for me.
I'm Gonna Be all I can be!

HI SKOOL HERE I COME

Ready to roll on the move
Hi Skool here I come.
Can't wait to start to play my part
Gonna make it lots of fun.

Shud b kool, Shud b gud,
The Skool still part of ma neighbourhood.
Looking forward to my first day.
Me and mi mates gonna make hay.

Still losing friends is not
Easy to do. Writing this
Rap am thinking of you.
To all of you who've
Been so kind; we'll meet
Again sum day sum time.

Am leaving Skool with memories,
On my way to the future.
Never liked all Skool activities,
Still a wanna say gud bye to the teachers.

For all the stress I must have caused, pushing chairs an
slamming doors.
In your desk leaving pests, chewing gum and apple cores.
Am ready to roll got my report.
Skool tie an shirt already bought.

Gonna be myself and nobody else.
With health, wealth,
And knowledge of self.

High Skool High Skool here I come.
Gonna make it shine wen things look glum.

Ready to roll on the move
High Skool here I come.
Can't wait to start to play my part
Gonna make it lots of fun.

TEXT TO A FRIEND

Don't be ignorant and watch time pass.
Digest your lessons while you're in class.
Being the class jester is like wasting fuel,
When you could be a precious Jewel.

This is the page you've got to read.
For all the lessons you'll truly need.
It's up to you to buckle down.
Unless you plan to be a circus clown.
Settle down and work through all the gears.
These are the words for both your ears.
Only you can do it for yourself,
But if you're stuck just ask for help.

Your brain is like a unique computer.
Built and designed just to suit ya.
To yourself please never deceive.
To tell yourself you can't achieve.
These are the lines you need to read.
For all the lessons you'll truly need.

Lessons bring knowledge, wisdom and skills.
And help you later to pay your bills.
You'll be able to do the things you like.
Education!
Not blackberries;
Makes your future bright.

Note: Jamaican proverb: Puddin can't bake wid out fire =
you need the right tools for the job.

ROLE LIKE ME

{Be all you can be}
R to the O to the L to the E
Can you role just like me.
M to the O. To the D.E.L
Role models help; you do well.

Like read and write and learn to spell,
To be on time when you hear the bell,
And if things do sometimes go wrong,
They'll be the first one to help you to write a new song.

Be loud and proud of who you are.
Manners and discipline will take you far.
A rolling stone will not gather moss,
If you don't believe me, just ask a boss.

It can be achieved with lots of work.
Like if you want to dig a hole, then you've got to dig
the dirt.
Now see you later or even next week.
And bless your socks you're so unique.
Well now I've had my chance to speak.
This little page is going to sleep.

DRINK SOME THINK

Beware of abuse from yourself.
To live a long life take care of your health.

Beware of slow poison in rusty bottles,
Beware beware it starts with a tottle.
Beware of spirits that come in many colours,
They lie in wait for you under covers.

Got to keep fit, stay in shape,
Too much booze and you may never wake.
Too much spirits will make you shake,
People have died in fermented lakes.

Alcohol, Beer, Wine, Spirits and Liqueur.
Will slowly dissolve away your liver.
Make you ill, some won't get better,
It shouldn't happen to you,
I know you're clever.

Even your blood and heart can suffer,
Simply because you didn't bother
To listen to the things you were told,
Too much alcohol will leave you cold.
Quickly grow old and rolled to mould.

Nothing should be done before the time,
Your body should be an adult,
Before you drink wine,

Alcohol, Beer of all type and sort.
Or you'll end up like a ship, at sea without a port.

So put this down in your own report,
To share your knowledge of what you've been taught.

WISE ADVICE

Wordz are for everyone and that's yhall too.
You're gonna have a go at something new.
Hear my advice and listen real good.
Keep your heads with the wise when you're in my
neighbourhood.
If you're a FAM,
A Cuz,
Or even a Blud,
YO! All I wanna do is to spread a little love.
So you all should know how risspek should be.
R.E.S.P.E.C.T!
Never diss a teacher you know they want to help ya.
Just tek a little breather and all will b cool.
And please don't act like you've never been to school.
My brain's so fly am gonna take you high.

My future's a rappster driving in my limo.
Aint gonna be a gangster I ain't no dimmo.
I don't hang out wid Snoop, Shaun, Paul or Shaggy.
But to my Kidz, I'm still the Tuff Daddy!

*Note: Yhall = all of you. Blud = Family or friend. Tek = Take.
Diss = Disrespect*

118

WOMAN

Oh mama, mama so pure,
Oh mother, women mek wi life it secure.
Oh mama, **the pain you endure**.
Oh mama mama we need you for sure.

Oh I say with **sincerity**.
Some forget what a woman should strive to be.
I'm not saying you can't be macho like me.
But do not lose your femininity.
I often wonder what it would be like.
One thing for sure the balance wouldn't be right.

Imagine; women on the streets picking fights.
Women in clubs throwing lefts and rights.
You should hear the things some of them utter.
To look at their face their mouth wouldn't melt butter.

A radiant face of an earth angel.
But her tongue is in a league with the beast in hell.
It's not a must to cuss, fuss, play tuff ruff.
Let us alleviate to communicate.

You all have a chance to be **a princess**.
Or do you want to be wicked witch of the west.
We all mek **mistakes** to be corrected.
Pray tell me why so much anger is vented.

WOMEN MOTHER OF CIVILISATION.
SHOW YOUR RESPONSE TO YOUR NATION.

We all came here from the womb.
You cared for us when there was no room.
You gave us **life** and a chance to **live**.
For this I know man is privileged.

Command **respect** with every step.
Move with pride and **etiquette**.
You are a **secret** men will want to discover.
Make him your prince is he respects your honour.

The time has come to **represent**.
Let the words from your mouth state your intent.

Don't lose the foundation of your ancestors.
You burn your **roots** the tree will wither.
Don't let the dirt outside tarnish the beauty within.
Do mi a beg you please just remember something.
If you continue or want to gwarn like a **jinal**.
Then you will always be **just a gyal**.
If you feel to grow diverse and wild.
Then who will guide the next lost child.

Oh mama, mama so pure,
Oh mama mama we need you for sure.

Note: Jinal = Trickster / cheater}
Gyal = Common name for a girl / woman

Women are the Mothers of civilisation and if not for the women many of us would not have been born.
They should be greeted and treated like sisters, princesses and queens, which is what they are.

Xclusion...

School should be fun not confusion.
Sometimes it can end in disillusion.
Can we think or find a way a better conclusion,
Or it's detention, isolation and xclusion.

Now am gonna tell you bout xclusions.
Please take response for all your actions.
Racism's one type of situation.
The first thing you'll be is in isolation.

Disrespecting yo is only for fools.
You'll soon find yourself sitting on stools.
Some people smoke, some people fight,
While other people think that this is alright.
If you smoke it's your own condemnation.
Or maybe never heard; the recommendation.
Smoking still causes a lot of pollution,
This is also a reason for your xclusion.
Now you're missing out on your inclusion.

School should be fun not confusion.
Sometimes it can end in disillusion.
Can we think or find a way a better conclusion,
Or it's detention, isolation and xclusion.

Schools have rulez and regulations,
It's not about fools and segregations.
Some are sometimes bad, some are sometimes rude,
Some are sometimes abusive, nasty and crude.
A if you misbehave you're in a situation.
You'll have lots of time for some evaluation.

Now you're missing out on your inclusion,
Check the consequences of your xclusion.

School should be fun not confusion.
Sometimes it can end in disillusion.
Can we think or find a way a better conclusion,
Or it's detention, isolation and xclusion.

By DC and Brad mc Westborough High

CONSORTIUM FOR EDUCATIONAL EXCELLENCE
A   R.A.P.   INITIATIVE

APPLICATION FORM 4da POET
DONAVAN CHRISTOPHER

Consortium Member: St Miscellaneous Grammar School
4 Boyz n Girlz
Initiative   3Rs Master Class, Rap, Reason,
Rhyme.

Clients: Name and contact address just in case we make a mess.
Address: A suit or bright-coloured attire, he always turns up in what he desires.
Contact: Trevor or speak to Paul, send for Rappaman it's fun for all.
Client Tel. Number: Is always a very good thing to remember.

Date of Initial Planning Meeting: As to discuss what the poet will be teaching, eating, sleeping or leaving.
Attended by: A consultant author from Space, have no fear he's of human race.

Why is the poet in need? To celebrate diversity and plant sum seeds,
To give cultural direction to children in need.

Description of project what will he do: Introduce your children to something new, break down barriers and deal with issues, every School has a possible few.
Through poetry, rap, rhyme and reason, send them to me and I will teach um, About themselves and other people,
Rap simply stands for Respect All People!

Aims of the project: To give them wisdom to protect, and challenge racism and disrespect, and to write nuff Raps about these things, and build a better world for us to all live in.
To provide some time to improve literacy skills,
And to keep um positive when they have time to kill.

Objective of the project: To give them in and external support about what they think they know and what they are taught, to raise esteem and keep um clean,
So a brighter future can be seen.

Outcomes of the project: The children will have more respect about the things they should not forget.
Intended plans for dissemination are:
Follow up work must be done to remind them that poetry is always FUN!
Ask the children to express their raps,
To the School assembly or to another class.

Any additional information:
DONAVAN CHRISTOPHER
R.A.P.P
RHYTHMIC AFRICAN PEACE POET
AKA: RAPPAMAN
REPORT IT TO SORT IT, I WILL SUPPORT IT.

Date(s) of project: As soon as the Schools call, email or text,
As sure as a fact the dates will be set.
Start: A.S.A.P **Finish:** All good things must come to an end.

Age/Year Group: All key stages   **No of participants:** T.B.A

Where project will take place: School classrooms and corridors or if it's free we'll use da hall.
Bless your home the family and Schools. It's where the kids learn the rulez.

WID NUFF RISSPEK IN ALL ASPECT
DC THE RAPPAMAN
Live an direct...

Canbefound.com   nothardtofind.co.uk

Answers to read an seek puzzles
How did you do?

In the Risspek Apartment:
Consider your litter = Hidden message is, Don't Drop Litter

In the Short Story Apartment
Last Books I read = Jonah and the Whale or Moby Dick/ Treasure Island/Perseus and the Medusa/Harry Potter and the Philosopher's Stone/Rappaman/The Demon Headmaster/ Peter Pan/The Lion, the Witch and the Wardrobe/Book of Rooms.

Lost word = The lost word is **Sorry** referring to lines 32,33,34,35 and 36 of the poem.

Another tale: This is narrated from the horse's point of view. Here are a few lines for sure. The title could have been spelt **Another Tail** a small clue.

3rd line of the poem, 'I hearken to Bess a sound I hear it's time for me to race'. Bess is the horse's name.

6th line of the poem, 'with leather clad around my back', refers to a saddle.

19th line of the poem refers to spurs in the horse's sides.

29th line of the poem, 'I was short of speech so stamped my feet'. This is what a horse can do to draw your attention.

There are many more to be found if you read and seek, please have fun discussing and exploring.

Hidden message in Another Tale = Straight from the horse's mouth.

Teaser for you to Fathom:
What can you take to another town or city but it never moves?

Joke 4 ya: Three horses in a field, one was called Pardon, one was called Pardon Pardon. And the other was called Pardon Pardon Pardon.

Sadly Pardon Pardon died. And Pardon Pardon Pardon died. Who was left? When they give you the answer, repeat the joke but don't smile.

> Now you get it.
> You smiled!

Answer to teaser = The roads!

Nuff respect for your support, I hope you remember what you've been taught.
Bless you, the family too and all the places you pass through.